COSMIC VISIONS

ISBN: 9798564017039

Cosmic Visions

Stuart Watkins

This is my second self-published work, after 'A United Kingdom' – Trains of Logical Thought which was released in June 2019, less than two weeks before I lost my beloved mother to cancer.

Many of the collections and arrangements of words in this book, (some use the word 'poems' to describe such pieces), date back a while. Others appeared much more recently. You have to go with the flow when relying on randomly generated texts produced by illiterate animals.

So it is what it is.

The artwork:

1. The Rainbow Metatron. The concentric circles are of the secondary colours Magenta, Yellow and Cyan and the perfectly positioned blanket is a white Metatron, which is an image from sacred geometry.

2. The Tree of Three. The symmetrical tree contains three hidden beings, a stag's skull, a woman throughout the centre and a slant-eyed demon with a long snout pointing downwards.The scarlet Celtic knot at the top is the Triquetra.

3. Pan's Pentagram. This incarnation has the Yin-Yang symbol at Spirit, and the Eye of Horus at it's centre. I like to think it protects me from the Pandemic.

All images are copyright protected.

The Unusual Writing Process

With the intention of creating a fresh piece of work requiring a minimum of personal effort, I decided to use the well-known "Infinite Number of Monkeys" theorem. The theorem states that if an infinite number of monkeys were to sit with an infinite number of typewriters, they would eventually write all existing literary works. The Complete Works of Shakespeare is the usual example given. Obviously new masterpieces would also appear.

Therefore, I recruited an infinite number of monkeys, and acquired - borrowed, out of financial necessity - an infinite number of laptops, and set them to work.

After some considerable time, many weeks in fact, having randomly created many famous texts including Wuthering Heights, Hermann Hesse's The Glass Bead Game, The Cat In The Hat, The Lord Of The Rings and Don Quixote, not to mention the brand new Shakespeare masterpiece (Queen) "Victoria", this far simpler accidental creation came to be. I had genuinely expected it to take much longer.

Stuart Watkins, February 2021

Contents

A Cosmic Vision

2020.

Clouds of death.
Rivers of death.
Fields of death.
Mountains of death.
Deserts of death.
Seas of death.
Streets of death.

Also, almost unimaginable magnitudes of money changing hands.

Also, almost unfathomable duplicity for personal financial gain, in the face of global human suffering. A candy shop for sweet-toothed "entrepreneurs", especially if they have the Right friends........

Rarely has there been such raw and and ruthless opportunism in our lifetimes, the **masks** and disguises of the commercial and political operations create themselves on this one...as do the profits behind the prophets.

The reminders, and remainders, of networks of unearned, assumed, secretive privilege. Of murky, misplaced, masculine, Masonic self-importance.

Many people have more intellect in a teeny, tweeny, tiny toe than in the mind of a pretender, a make-believe Old Etonian Walter Mitty, or perhaps a prissy, priapic prima donna, hand on cock, crying like the proverbial crocodile in front of a colostomic camera.

A veritable world-beating government team worthy of Alf Ramsay and Bobby Moore's conquerors of 1966, and no mistake. They ooze professionalism, pride, integrity and honesty, ugly nationalism, money, greed and corruption. Those things have an unmistakable odious odour. In my humblest of opinions. Impressions can be deceptive and incorrect though, which means that one can easily trust, and even employ, the wrong PR gurus and experts sometimes. Moulding the attitudes and beliefs of Joe Public can be in the lap of the gods, even for the most talented of manipulators and deceivers.

....

Yet, simultaneously, authentic heroes and heroines battled and fought for others, friends and family, complete strangers, tirelessly, putting themselves and their own lives at the very lowest priority, because to them it is about fellow human beings. That's not a concept that everyone understands. It creates the vision of an upside-down pyramid, where the wrong people are at the top and the wrong people are at the bottom, and one needn't be a mathematical genius to realise that such a pyramid would fall over, because it's dysfunctional and makes no sense that way up.

Unviable, a cut-throat narcissistic sociopath might call it. We know of a few of those.

We have been united in, and by, our humanity, for the most part. Certainly both the very best and the very worst of human characteristics have been on wide-open display, it has been pathetic and hilarious in equal measure when the effect has been the opposite of the intention. Incompetence, apathy and swimming-out-of-depth have been commonplace in high office, unfortunately.

We've been together through extreme highs and lows, seeing sporadic jubilation, but also sadly widespread grief and personal pain and calamity. Our eyes startled, shocked, exhausted and overwhelmed. There have been such moving stories of courage and altruism. Alongside them, crushing examples of horrific, psychopathic profiteering. For example, it is supposed to be illegal, in principle, to make investments where they can be under your control or influence, in most instances it constitutes "insider trading". I don't think it too much to ask that politicians should have to declare any holdings in, say, a pharmaceutical company making millions of doses of a vaccine that the public purse will be paying for. Hypothetically of course. Be that investment direct or indirect, through an intermediary or a third party or a limited company perhaps. That's not an accusation, just an observation. It seems possible. Feasible. Just elementary critical thinking and logic, you know?

Anybody that particular cap fits, is in a safe, protected place because there is no compulsion for such information to be shared. They know who they are. And the All-Seeing Eye, that Freemasons are supposed to recognise and serve, sees them too.

....

The social media platforms.

Their precious, populist pretence of the power of participation, and their deafening white noise of trivial, transitory traffic, and their smokescreens of deviousness and deception, and their unaccountable autonomy, and their narratives of negativity and nothingness, consume and cover the addicted, asphyxiated, anxiety-drenched, apoplectic user population with invisibility cloaks, worthy of any wizard, warlock or witch.

They are only, just like your friendly, trusted, printed and broadcast media;

Factories of distraction.
Engines of illusion.
Creators of confusion.
Dungeons of delusion.
Mines and machines of marauding, manipulative misinformation.
Labyrinths of lies.

Tabloids full of taxidermic, totalitarian, trashy, organised, obtuse and obstructive opinions.

11

Facts are in intentionally, deliberately short supply, conspicuous by their absence.

As an analogy, the apparent, amiable assistance and protection of the fireproof asbestos, is rapidly replaced and substituted with crippling, creeping and crushing suffocation, by its invading, insidious fibres and splinters.

....

Once upon a time, we were each a zealous, zestful zygote, in oceans of oestrogen and prototypal progesterone, topographic tales of testosterone, a lascivious and lecherous lottery of gregarious and gangrenous gender games and gambles. A chromosome cocktail.

I spew my spidery spleen and my sparse, spellbound, spluttering spirit into space, through a dreary, deep, dark prism of desolate, destructive, deathly doorways.

A terrifying triptych - temptingly tessellated, though torn by the clustered claret claws and twisted talons of time's tornado.

The soup of micro-organisms in the sacred Ganges, its flames of purifying force on the pyres of Varanasi, the ever-eternal and immortal venom of Set, course through our bodies as cleansing energies and illuminate our celestial pathways.

In the grotto of occult wisdom sits the Astroscope. It rests among the mighty, majestic, magnificent, magickal, mystical, masterful, mythical, marvellous, mysterious, metaphysical, massive branches and boughs of the World Tree, the legendary Yggdrasil.

My Cosmic Visions, the Coy, Vain, Critical Veins of my Cold, Vacant Curriculum Vitae, in this age of the Callous, Vengeful Corona Virus.

Andromeda's Fire

Look upon me and see me as a ghost
of past messengers, trustworthy and true;
sweeping, arching rainbows spraying colour,
encircling my essence and towering into the blue.

Crush and mould and bastardise the elements,
stark volcanic granite into blankets of flower;
microscopic particles to arrows of spite,
piercing the mind and drilling, by minute and by hour.

Am I alive or dead, or spreading through the all,
sickle and scythe through a tapestry of barley,
harvesting optimism, fields clear for growth and hope,
massacre and mercenary, march of the new army.

Cages of straw imprison the raven and the dove,
opening sources of peaceful, flowing emptiness;
batter and splice it, optical illusion
deceives but then reverses, more becomes less.

Gallows stand, anticipate the mob
who lynch and bay, pretenders to a force above.
Blood, sweat and urine merge as ambrosia,
powerless rhythm diameter to the wave of love.

Typhoon blizzard burning from the chasm,
abyss of demonic lava so wide and deep;
tearing at the flesh of Olympian idols,
Rosicrucian Trinity shadowing the Lord of Sleep.

We can feel turning, a dervish spin –
latitudes as a ladder in banded space;
wings of butterflies reverberate
to the peak of sensibilities in the psychic race.

Hermits stranded in a cosmic sphere
tapping arteries, kaleidoscope of crystal view,
explosions shatter to illuminate,
fireflies torch the air and lead us through.

Gates of infinity, ecstatic maelstrom cloud,
friend and foe as one, the shameful and the proud;
white is black, war is peace, whispers loud,
joy splashes through, lifeforce binds the crowd.

Old Man

Sometimes in the morning when the sun rises,

in the evening after a heavy day,

when tumbling promises break apart loudly,

walls and floors buckling like clay.

The Old Man

at the windmill,

I talk to him.

He tells me stories that take my troubles away.

When there are questions I need to ask

to see and hear the secrets of Earth,

when all has deserted me cruelly,

when I wonder what everything is worth;

The Old Man

at the castle,

I speak with him.

He laughs with me and fills my heart with truth.

Life's jigsaw pieces scattered on the floor,

how am I to start to piece them together?

The hermit's vision is unpolluted,

he sees the elements create the weather.

The Old Man

at the sea,

he tells me.

I leave his company with thoughts I keep forever.

Spirits encircle us, but remain unseen,

light and dark through tunnels of thought;

difficult choices, which to grasp,

wires of temptation stretched and taut.

The Old Man

in the sky,

knows them all.

He smiles and shares wisdom from a timeless heart.

Drifting into parallel dimensions,

sights and colours take my breath away;

spiritual flights beyond the material,

triumphant gardens where children play.

The Old Man,

he lives there,

he shows me.

I feel belief that brings a brand new day.

The Old Man speaks to me all the time,

the voice of reason from the astral plane.

He is a very good friend of mine,

a calming presence on a runaway train.

The Old Man

within me,

he holds me.

Cradling my soul to shield it from pain.

The Old Man waits there for you and me,

telling magical stories we can believe.

Guiding light from the spirit world,

weaver of the perfect weave;

The Old Man

knows us,

loves us.

Join with his spirit and feel it breathe.

The Old Man is a mountain of love.

The Old Man is a fountain of light.

The Old Man burns in the rising sun.

The Old Man's shadow is the dead of night.

That Old Man,

that young boy,

that spirit,

shining and blinding, ecstasy bright.

Friend

I know you're always there, friend.
It makes me sure,
it makes me strong.
I know you're everywhere, friend.
I've known it all along.

I need you when I'm down, friend.
To lift me up
and make me smile.
It helps when you're around, friend
to rescue this small child.

Sometimes when life is hard, friend,
I'm glad you're there
to help me through,
a message or a card, friend,
reminds me I have you.

And when you need a friend, friend,

I'm always here,

I promise you.

Until the very end, friend,

I'm always here for you.

Mother

As you sit there, about to lose your mother,

it's as if she physically draws, and pulls —

with power but with delicate subtlety —

each single teardrop, from deep within your very soul.

Her eyes are closed.

Her heartbeat is faint.

And your spirit melts

into those tears of agony.

Every vivid, beautiful memory is

of days of joy,

of days of sorrow,

days of love

and days of trust.

The fearful anticipation of that very final moment

when she slips away from the world.

. . . .

And when she does,

when that final flood of tear-water

cascades into a hollow nowhere,

there is release.

Relief.

The letting go.

The half-smile that automatically appears,

when the inner goodbye

full of love and remembrance comes,

is not painful.

She has permission to leave.

Never again will there be

a bitter or angry thought,

only complete appreciation

of everything she was,

and still is,

memories that cannot be touched.

Everything she was, and still is, remains, for ever.

Questions?

Is the ocean blue-ish green or green-ish blue?
Is the sky still blue at night or is it black?
Does a politician lie or tell it true?
Does the pusher sleep well after selling smack?

Why does a moth dance into a flame?
Do seagulls dream of the lives of fish?
Can a child's tortoise recognise its own name?
Does it help if it's written on its dish?

Who invented the concept of games and sport?
Who started the trend for suicide?
Is it true that a soul can be sold or bought?
Will we all find out the answer when we've died?

Is patience a virtue, what about faith and hope?
Do cameras and mirrors tell lies?
Does the thin end of the wedge start a slippery slope?
Who cares what happens to spies?

Some questions have answers, others do not.

There are probably more but I think I forgot.

The Zenith

I

Are we born in a box
with complicated locks?
Hardwired from birth
to wander this Earth
in a particular way –
every innumerable, immeasurable day
for the whole of our lives?
Our husbands, our wives,
programmed, predetermined
in advance,
the inevitable and seductive dance
of inescapable fate.

II

Do our parents really name us?
Stuart, Stephen or Seamus,

did they, do I, have free will,

or simply climb our destined hill,

automatically,

carrying out an unwitting plan

devised by an omnipotent invisible man?

Why not a woman,

women seem as strong as men to me.

I am not speaking of cutting down a tree;

but the power of the immortal soul,

a man often half of a woman's whole.

Again — are our names even our own?

An organic part of our skin and bone?

Are our choices ours to effect

or just manifestations, circumspect?

III

Some believe in fate, in destiny,

each minute detail of the cosmogony,

the appearance of randomness and chaos

nothing but a mirage of a morass.

28

The overwhelming illusion of infinite choices

and their seemingly limitless voices,

offering hundreds of optional doors;

each offering thousands of inviting whores;

each offering millions of addictive, magnetic pills;

delivering billions of irresistible kills

of pasts.

And new births of lives,

trillions of bees from innumerable hives

swarming upward and skyward to space

as if in some vertical cosmic race.

Yet within one teardrop it is all contained,

merging into puddles, pools and streams,

as indistinguishable as shattered fragments of dreams,

they become one, like the sands of a desert,

unfathomably impossible to measure.

IV

In the soup in the swamp at the start,

were we mapped like a point on a chart?

29

Or is everything a vortex of chance?

A celestial, all-consuming dance,

where fluidity governs in ambiguity

through quantum dimensions of entropy.

V

In positive and negative space

is the wall or the window the base?

The Yin and the Yang in our souls,

are they observable only as holes?

Is the space or the matter what's real,

is there anything before which we should kneel?

VI

So we arrive at the notion of 'God',

which for many is absurdly odd.

Scientists pacing around

seeking birthday gifts to pass around,

in the face of 'blind faith',

30

the adversary, the weapon that confounds.

That catch-all excuse with no solution,

theory, devoid of conclusion.

There is the magnetism from a pair of eyes,

the pragmatism of a compromise.

The blackest abyss in the multiverse,

the bottomless pit of an evil curse.

A hideous fear in our psyche's depth.

The dread holds us fast in the dragon's breath.

Galaxies are in spin.

Magnets drag us in.

The velocity of light.

An abstract fight.

Esoteric pathways are revealed.

Ancient doorways are concealed.

Secret civilisations long past.

A pair of scales hang from a golden mast.

Gates to a realm from legend and lore.

Millennia since they were seen before.

Knowledge hidden since the birth of time,

deep in the heart of a concubine.

Consort of an emperor, owner of her soul,

exercising absolute and total control.

VII

Love.

The most powerful force in all of humanity.

It is a precipice over which we fall.......

there is nothing we can do about it at all

(nor do we wish to).

The most extreme power we ever experience,

a superlative Ragnarök of magnificence.

In general, prior warnings are not present,

all maps and directions are absent.

As we peer into the void of the drop,

not the slightest temptation to stop.

VIII

Some never get to feel it,
nor to beg, borrow or steal it.
Confusion and loss.
A Rubicon cross.
From a quantum design.
Oscillations align.
Chasms of black.
A nuclear attack.
A holocaust's cloud
annihilates the crowd.

The desolation, the vapour,
and the stench of scorched flesh,
that hangs from the crawling,
so deformed and appalling.
The melting cadavers
of mothers and fathers.
Screams, full of pain,
where ashes remain,

black bodies,

in flames,

no dignity or shame.

Decisions are taken.

Mankind forsaken.

Power enacted,

names – redacted.

IX

The Yellow Star.

The Red Giant.

The White Dwarf.

The Black Hole.

X

Love.

Some have the good fortune to encounter it once.

A rare, fortunate few

fall off multiple cliff edges.

34

And they feel the electricity of privilege

in their flesh, bones, minds and hearts.

If we seek out that precious Grail of life

it is nowhere to be found.

The only way it can be discovered

is for it to find us.

As elusive as a pretty blue butterfly when sought.

But, when least expected,

at the turn of the blindest of corners,

it will strike with the beautiful, deadly, sudden flash

of a rattlesnake.

No prior warnings are given,

no maps or directions are present.

Exactly as with the legendary, blissful agony of the

bite and kiss of a predatory, seductive vampire,

surrender is unquestioning and absolute.

Complete, welcome, rapturous ecstasy.

XI

That moment feels………

like the Universe itself has bestowed it upon us.

As if we have been primed for it for our whole lives.

We have been waiting for it

without even knowing what it is.

Oblivious of it, yet immediately upon its arrival,

recognising it like a long-lost brother, or sister.

So, it is an inexpressible tragedy

that there are souls, worthy of love,

that live their entire lives yet never enter that realm

of the all-encompassing loss

of every nuance of control.

And so I arrive at the answer to my question.

XII

How can we be born into a box

held fast and secure with complicated locks

if the very focus,

the very target,

the very pinnacle,

the very destination,

the most life-affirming discovery,

the most sublime secret,

our purpose,

the very zenith of our

existence and experience

is a random occurrence?

Some never find it at all

while others find it more than once,

and so..........

We can only deduce that if that

ocean of perfection

is only arbitrarily discovered,

we must be endowed with our own free will,

and randomness and chaos are also in play.

No grand design, no grand designer.

Chameleon

Chameleon masquerades as the bringer of peace,
ever the visionary, begging release.
Chameleon masquerades as peasant or poet,
the disguise can deceive but some will know it.
Chameleon hides among heroes and men,
unites and unsettles weaker brethren.
Chameleon masquerades with consummate skill,
if one face does not convince the next surely will.
Chameleon's eyes burn with Satan's flame
and with laughter, as he plays his game.

Chameleon masquerades as a shooting star,
slashing the night as an image afar.
Chameleon's colours are vivid and bright,
rainbow intruder in desperate night.
Chameleon dances to a furious drum,
crescendo of celestial momentum.
Chameleon contorts into a twisted knot –
the memories of Sodom, the anguish of Lot.

Chameleon masquerades as woman and man,
Hermaphroditus sips from Salmacis' fountain.

Chameleon blushes, imitates Fire,
igniting his soul with the heat of desire.
Chameleon drinks of the Water of life,
mimics the tension between husband and wife.
Chameleon encrusts with elemental Earth,
calls into question his self and his worth.
Chameleon soars on an angel's wings,
Chameleon pretends he's a thousand things.

Orgasmo

Touch

    Relax

        Free

           Warm

                Move

              Feel

                Wet

                Fire

              Fly

                Drift

                  Soar

                      Dream

Psycho-Espionage

Inside your thoughts
and wild imaginations
I can feel what you feel
experience your situations.

Through a life of doubt
to awakenings and visions
a surgeon of the mind
precise incisions.

Footsteps in the corridor
over your shoulder
in your private rooms
younger and older.

In the wanderings of sleep
when you hum a song
you can feel me there
my presence is strong.

41

To the edge of time
we will run and fly
some times we'll laugh
others we'll cry.

Open the well of your soul
let me pour in water
wisdom can flow like a river
or die like a martyr.

We'll shoot like a fireball
to a magical place
share the consciousness of all
see the Master's face.

Do you feel me calling you
through the blackness of space?
A spy, through your open eye,
without a tangible trace.

The Golfin' Dolphin

There once was a crazy little dolphin
who decided he would try a spot of golfin'.
He thought that he might not be very good,
but when the others went, he said he would.

At the first tee he stood up straight and tall,
and swung – but I'm afraid he missed the ball!
He tried again and hit off for the green....
perhaps it was the worst shot ever seen.

He practised on and on throughout the day,
(and gradually got better, by the way).
He practised more and more from week to week,
until he was quite useful, so to speak.

Well now he is the Champion of the World.
Knows every shot, the straight one and the curled.
He mixes with the famous men and women,
and owns a great big pool for which to swim in!

A dolphin who will be recalled in history.

Quite how he did it will remain a mystery.

Perhaps there'll never be another dolphin

that beats the world through practising his golfin'.

Space

To lose control and bare my soul,
to find my own essence in a flake of snow,
to feel the Dragon's breath in my heart
and see it in each tree and field;
the space I occupy
is as imaginary as Time itself.

Watching the light of each burning star,
eclipsed by sailing vapours on the ice-winds,
the rising sun is warm and hopeful
and greets the mists of dawn;
this space drifts by
leaving emptiness in its wake.

Flashes of storm-sky crack the night air
as snakes snapping to trap their prey,
sweet venom and blood mingling
like evil with blind innocence;

space opens wide

to welcome all dreams and fears.

In all spasms of bright joy and spirit

which deceive the spineless worm-laughter,

ascent into stratospheric orbit

above all precious beauty shining;

a space within a space,

bathing and basking in sunbeams.

The Night Owl

I

Ah! What was that!

I awaken, there must have been a noise.

The slam of a car door,

the low, gruff bark of a substantial dog,

or perhaps the shriek of a frightened cat.

Possibly a bang from my neighbours' side of the wall.

I glance at the clock at my bedside

in the pitch blackness

at the red LED image.

It's 3.12am.

No sooner is my head resting again on the soft pillow

than I am drifting away,

as if I had never awakened at all.

II

I am in a house. it's tall.

it seems to have a number of floors

and many rooms, maybe twenty rooms.

It has five or six storeys if one includes the cellar.

I feel younger.

I know where I am

and I know where this is.

It's Oxford, in December,

I'm at university,

as if it were yesterday.

As if it were today.

Right here, and right now.

The house is full of student party,

I smell the unmistakable

cannabis and tobacco,

the cheap wine and beer,

and there is more than a hint of vomit
in this particular room as well.

Someone has unfortunately misjudged
their capacity to abuse their body.
The sweat, and the resulting stench
of collective body odour,
of the sheer volume of unwashed students
that occupy every tiny space and corner
of every room.
It's a miasma of decadence and stupor.

But where is my girlfriend, Michelle?

I know we arrived here together.
It's a party though, and so I need to explore the place
to find out which of the twenty or so rooms
she has wandered into.

III

As I weave in and out of the rooms
I overhear discussions,
giving expert analysis of Plato's Republic,
or expert analysis of Einstein's Theory of Relativity,
or expert analysis of Da Vinci's polymathic genius,
or expert analysis of the creativity of Lloyd Wright.
Expert analysis of the work of Stephen Hawking
or Chaucer's Canterbury Tales.

Perhaps the exhaustive and inspired
works of William Shakespeare,
of Dante's Inferno, or Poe, or Lovecraft.

Analysis of the slaughter of Native Americans,
or the unworkability of communism,
or the unworkability of capitalism.
(Although the interference of human nature
always causes the psychology of greed
to usurp the philosophy of the theory,

50

and the ideals to be warped and ruined).
I take a look around me.

To the Left of me, Red Clowns.
To the Right, Blue Jokers.
I feel stuck in the middle with.....
but where are you, Michelle?
I feel stuck in the middle without you.
Only the clowns and the jokers in sight.

Thoughts still penetrate my cranium
and randomly flood my brain.
Intellectual critiques of the art
of Van Gogh, Picasso and Rembrandt;
Dali, Magritte and their surreal and abstract statements.
Banksy's audacious sabotage and destruction
of his own creation, at public auction.
The aesthetic splendour
of Barbara Hepworth and Paul Klee.

Expert explanations

of the properties of all the chemical elements

of the Periodic Table, and all the theory

that governs how they are arranged;

why they all have their individual numbers,

and places, and how all roots of Chemistry

begin with them.

The 'ins' and the 'outs'

of quantum mechanics.

Thermodynamics.

Superstring theory,

the advanced idea of extra dimensions

on which that rests.

Expert examination of belief systems,

of religions, of atheism,

of the efforts to control minds.

Of the fact that later religious doctrines

have their origins in ancient civilisations.

That long before the 'one God', the monotheism,

came the notion of multiple gods

of Egypt and Greece

and Rome and Scandinavia.

The quest for the truth in that mess of ideas,

consumes my subconscious for what seems

to be minutes, but is probably only seconds.

All of a sudden I hear music.

It seems to be just a morass of motifs.

It seems to be a million tunes,

all playing at once

yet I can distinguish between them all.

From Gregorian chants by monks

to Albinoni, Beethoven, Chopin, Dvorak and Elgar,

Pink Floyd, Genesis, Yes and Led Zeppelin,

The Beatles, Abba, Miles Davis, the Spice Girls!

Heated debates full of shouts and yells
are raging about
"who is the greatest drummer of all time?"
Cobham? Moon? Rich? Bruford? Portnoy?

Colaiuta? Bonham? Harrison? Donati?

Then the guitarist argument kicks in:
Holdsworth? Di Meola? Segovia?
Vai? Gilmour? Petrucci?

Then as suddenly as it arrived,
the entire musical dimension is gone.

Mathematics introduces itself.
The insights of Ptolemy and Eratosthenes,
and of Galileo, Copernicus.
The riddle of Fermat's Last Theorem,
that baffled mathematicians for 358 years.
The infinite perfection of Pi,
and Phi, and the Golden Ratio,

and the Fibonacci series,

and the ultimate beauty of numbers,

all flood through this dreamy psychospace.

IV

The theoretical is replaced by the visual

and I am in a crowded space in a London pub.

I am in the presence of loud, offensive people

that I at first assume are inebriated

football fans, until I realise

that they are yelling about.....

Brexit.

I can detect some key comments;

it seems the EU are out for power.

They want to enslave the British people

whilst giving complete freedom to

all other EU states.

Brits want to sever connections to Brussels

because people in Brussels are evil,

and worship Satan,

despite the fact that Satan is imaginary.

The English language is to be abolished

and systematically phased out.

It seems everybody in the EU will be compelled by law

to speak French and/or German only,

because France and Germany are taking over.

First Europe and then the rest of the world.

But this was apparently leaked out,

so everybody became aware of it,

and a man named "NF" Farage, rhymes with garage,

saved the whole country by making people

hate EU states

and EU citizens

and everything about the EU.

All the things that appeared good about the EU

were apparently all fake,

it was all a big plot to deceive people

that thought unity was better than division,

Division, as we now know,

is better than unity.

Doubt far better than trust.

I don't like what I'm hearing

in this horrible, smelly place.

It's very uncomfortable.

It all just sounds like lies.

There's a door to my right, my Far Right,

that seems to have sensible

business people in it.

I move within earshot.

It seems they are talking about money.

This Brexit,

it means that things like

imports and exports

can all be realigned and renegotiated.

Smell that money!

The EU laws about such things

favour our sworn enemies

France and Germany.

The huge amount of money

that Britain has to pay to the EU,

that has "no benefit to Britain at all",

we can keep!

Yes!

Money!

Now, I am sitting in a wood-panelled room,

around a big mahogany table,

everyone is wearing suits

and name badges.

The badges are adorned

with little photographs of their wearers

and their titles.

Which government department they work in.

No information at all about who they work FOR.

Invisible people.

Non-existent identities.

Banknotes line the walls

and drop out of holes in the ceiling,

while all the suits grin,

psychopathically,

sociopathically,

mindlessly.

They study the agenda for the meeting,

the Brexit fallout,

the Brexit benefits to whomever,

and they giggle mercilessly.

they self-identify as the 'Great British Freedom Fighters'.

The self-same nationalist blind men

are referred to by the people with human values

as the 'Brain Dead Imbecile Club',

though sadly they are not really imbeciles.

Their thoughts and actions are intentional.

And calculated.

V

My dream is gone in a flash.

Suddenly it's a different office, different men.

You don't see women in this gathering.

Women allow emotions into

the most inappropriate situations,

it's safer to keep them out.

The accents are no longer the Queen's English,

but American.

Northern accents, Southern accents,

Western accents, Eastern accents.

One of the names mentioned is Hillary Clinton,

another is Donald Trump,

another is Robert Mueller,

another is Dan Bongino.

I do a little Googling,

I see a talk given by Mr. Bongino.

There seems to be a can of different worms

to those of the Brexit shenanigans,

but they seem to be equally horrible worms.

The rabbit holes -

like the One offered to Neo in The Matrix -

seem very real as I listen to the extracts I find.

The "Russian collusion", was it Clinton, not Trump?

Both? About different things?

Never mind the White Rabbit,

follow the uranium.

You can seemingly buy anything

with enough money,

from rare trace elements to the souls of people.

Allegedly.

As I listen, I'm spooked.

There are always Spooks.

VI

Another flash, I'm gone.

The politicians and wood-walled rooms are gone.

I'm back at the house party,

With drugged-up students and no offices or suits.

The CONversations are therefore

once again CONcerning the

CONtemplation of navels,

mixed with intellectual pretenders

putting the world to rights

as if they were able to, from a wooden room.

Some students are CONvinced they know

everything there is to know,

plus, of course,

things that are not known

or even able to be known.

Then there are others,

with sponge-like open minds.

Because of this,

conversations propagate

in the smoky, druggy rooms

of "student-houseparty-world".

As for me, in my dream,

because I want to be an arrogant educator

and an open-minded sponge

at the same time,

I flutter, like a butterfly,

between all the rooms in the house,

uttering, and stuttering,

and pontificating,

and solving the world's problems.

Learning and teaching simultaneously.

Indulging in the intense cosmic discourse

without remembering a single word of it all.

But where's Michelle?

She's back again

in the forefront of my awareness.

All of the rooms

have numbers on them,

because it is a student-house,

meaning that it has been divided

into as many monetisable units
as possible.

I had overheard, perhaps,
four or five such conversations
in each of the bedrooms I had ventured into.

While putting the state of the world
and random dissonant matters
into perspective, under a
philosophical microscope,
I gradually consume
enough cheap wine and beer
to lose my awareness of everything around me.
I am still verbally pushing and pulling
but it is all now on auto-pilot,
so I have no clue what I am hearing or saying.

It is probably drivel.
What I am hearing is probably drivel
and what I am saying is probably drivel,

because we are thoroughly inebriated

and as high as fucking kites.

Somebody then accuses me

of ripping them off in a computer game,

to the tune of twenty English guineas.

Somebody else's girlfriend accuses me

of the improper suggestion

that she and I carry out some obscene acts

in front of a webcam.

What's a webcam?

Will this challenge end in a deadly, digital duel?

VII

My memory is full of broken half-thoughts by now,

so I cannot remember what I said to anybody,

nor can I recall whether I even played a video game.

Then, I again remember that I arrived with Michelle,

so I stand up,

at the fourth attempt

after three dismally inept efforts,

and begin to explore once again.

Although, other than her,

everyone in the house is a complete stranger,

each with a forgettable and unfamiliar face,

the deep and meaningful discussions

of the last however long

enable me to recognise people

in most of the rooms.

I will have told them my name

("Ambrose" was my usual party pseudonym)

and they will have told me theirs

(either the real or the invented),

yet I will not have remembered

any of those identifiers.

Just like I cannot remember

any of the content

of anything I've talked about.

So I decide to be systematic -

and search for Michelle from cellar to attic -

which should be less problematic -

and almost automatic -

especially since my senses are severely impaired

due to the chemical cocktail in my blood.

I find her! In a room with the number 13 on the door,

which for a few brief moments

plays havoc with my triskaidekaphobia,

but it passes quickly

as I am too disengaged for coherent thought.

I sit with her,

she is in a similar state of mind.

So rather than attempt anything cerebral,

we giggle, talk gibberish,

and choose not to move for a while.

VIII

However.

You know how it is

when you can sense imminent rain?

The slight change in humidity,

the moisture on the very air?

The most subtle alterations in

the sensation of the surroundings?

Well.

As we sit there on the floor of Room 13,

and it makes no practical sense

to blame the number on the door,

but in that same way one can sense looming rainfall,

I was able to detect an ominous air of

portentous darkness and evil

at that moment.

In looking around me,

nothing physical had changed whatsoever.

Those endless unfamiliar faces.

Their conversations uninterrupted,

their number no greater or fewer,

their countenance oblivious to

the marauding presence.

There is something else about

the approaching danger.

Frequencies, vibrations,

at levels that my heart

is somehow able to interpret, and decipher,

and understand, tell me

that the precise and specific 'aim' of this threat

is to cut out my heart.

Yet it is my heart itself

that senses the motive of the threat,

even though the danger has,

at this point,

no physical manifestation or form.

Michelle and I help each other to our feet
and leave the house.
We step out into the extreme winter cold
and then, all of a sudden,
I am somewhere completely different.
Michelle has vanished into nowhere.

IX

I am tied fast to a metal pole.

My hands are fastened behind my back
and around the pole.

The pole is atop a hill, fifty or sixty metres high,
rising above a level plain.

There is an identical hill, of an identical height,
some eighty metres to my left.

My childhood best friend
is similarly bound to a metal pole at its summit.

There is a large gathering of spectators
around the two hills and, respectfully,
nobody stands on the slopes of the grassy domes;
instead, they congregate at the bottom, on the flat.

Torrential rain is falling.
Forks of lightning and huge thunderclaps abound.
In the next seconds, the lightning will
simultaneously strike the poles.

This is a double execution,
perpetrated by sheer force of nature.

The crime? Unauthorised thought processes.

As the baying of the crowd reaches fever pitch,
I prepare for the instantaneous
boiling of my blood

and melting of my eyes.

What will I feel, or will there not be enough time
to feel a thing?

X

At the exact moment of incineration,
as if being instantaneously transported
to a new astral plane
and sphere of consciousness
in a split-second,
I feel my body, mind and spirit
explode in excruciating white heat -
and suddenly I am conscious once again,
in the same shell
but with a brand new, fresh, activated soul.

I am moving.

The scenario is closest to,

though not all that close to,

the sensation of being in a car

at a point on a motorway,

in the dark, approaching a nameless city,

where bright, orange, sodium streetlights

whizz past at what seems every nano-second.

And then, in a moment, the lights disappear.

I am back at the house, but alone, 'sans-Michelle'

as if she were an island in France at high tide.

Although the darkness and its dense tangibility

have disappeared too,

I am equally terrified - because now,

I am being pursued by something different.

Something even worse.

And it is very close.

I am in the gravest danger.

The faces at the party are all different

from those I had seen earlier

and they are all focused on me.

At this most inconvenient of moments
I need to use the bathroom.
The cheap alcohol has filled my bladder to bursting
so I must obey the agonising command,
come what may.
There can be no escape route now.

Privacy is out of the question,
the bathroom is full of people.
I will have to urinate before spectators
though at this moment they appear uninterested,
though the mysterious, threatening mood
has not lessened for it.
I have to both relax and concentrate to do the deed
but it comes without any delay.

Afterwards, I appear to still exist.
I have to try and work out
exactly where the threat is coming from,

but that is impossible.

since it seems to be coming from everywhere.

There is no indication of any safe place anywhere.

It is all I can do to not just surrender rather than run

and let the chips fall where they may.

Then, I decide to at least leave the house,

as it is dripping with pure dread.

So I sprint down the flights of stairs

and out of the front door,

and then I am in a maze of city streets

which are totally unfamiliar,

yet somewhere in the back of my mind

there is a vague awareness of where this is.

XI

I just continue to run.

I don't know which direction helps me

and which is towards the horror that is pulling me,

it seems,

regardless of where I try to escape to,

there isn't anywhere to escape to.

I know that I will not evade what awaits me.

Yet I try, I run, from the unseen force.

It is as if it does not gain on me

but I cannot increase the distance between

it, and me, either.

As my resolve wanes and dies

and I become convinced I have no way out,

my logical neural pathways somehow connect

with my subconscious nightmare

and I remember I can fly.

I have flown in my dreams numerous times,

yet often I am not able to connect to it

and so cannot use the power,

but when the connection comes

it is as easy as walking.

I rise.

I rise above the fear.

I rise above the landscape.

I rise above the vision.

I rise to a level of control.

Now, I am in full command of this world.

I fly.

At first, vertical. Rapid.

As if I've snatched and grasped the guide rope

of a hot air balloon with no restraints.

Up. Up. Up. Up. Up.

Seconds before breaking out of

the Earth's atmosphere,

I switch to a horizontal trajectory

but maintaining projectile velocity.

I am free from 'whatever it was'.......

I continue to fly

for what seems maybe a hundred miles,

but in a very short span of time.

And then

I come back down to the surface of the Earth.

I'm in an English city.

One that I do not recognise individually,

but it has that 'English city' character

and comfortable familiarity.

Cheltenham, or Bath, or Royal Leamington Spa,

or Manchester, or Liverpool, or Shrewsbury.

I have been here before, but I haven't.

The landmarks aren't there.

It's as if my dream is taunting me,

making me guess where I am

but without all the clues.

No recognisable buildings,

no recognisable waterways or shorelines.

But it's unmistakably England.

It confuses me.

Where did I park my car?

Which of the many cars that I have owned in my life

is the one that I am searching for?

All concept of time is absent.

I don't know where I am

78

despite the air of familiarity.

I don't know when I am

as there is nothing to help me,

nothing by which to gauge my surroundings.

I calm myself down,

and begin to walk, and look around me.

Which car?

The BMW? The Mercedes? The Astra?

The Peugeot? The Renault? The VW?

Nothing specific will obey the attempt at recall.

It feels like limbo.

Recognising things, but not.

Feeling comfortable, but not.

Knowing where I am in time, but not.

Is it London?

Brent Cross?

Notting Hill?

Wimbledon?

Marylebone?

Again, I know it, but I don't.

XII

And then, slowly, deliberately,

my brain begins to settle,

much like the aftermath of a sandstorm,

with the wind having subsided,

so that all the airborne matter

can sink to the ground and coat it, like snow.

My thoughts begin to form, to crystallise.

It's a dream. No more, no less.

The line is crossed, in my thoughts,

bringing awareness, and calm,

and all doubt and fear is no longer with me, at all.

Very soon, I will be able to wake myself up

and my heart rate will settle down fully.

Before I wake myself

I wish to observe, explore the patterns of the streets.

The reason that I cannot isolate the exact location

is because my mind is still toying with me a little,

and the layout of the streets and roads

is an elaborate maze.

Dead ends. Blind corners.

Nothing that I recognise.

No matter where I go or where I look,

it's nowhere, it's nothing.

It bores me.

There isn't any point exploring

because it is an aimless quest,

there's just nothing to look for, nothing to find.

And so, all that remains

is to wake myself,

something I taught myself to do

some years ago, when I somehow managed

to reconnect my conscious and subconscious -

at moments of abject fear or terror -

in the depths of horrific nightmares -

when the first waves of my schizophrenia

introduced themselves to me.

Within the Dream

I lay my body down upon the tarmac of the road.

Within the Dream

I settle my thoughts and relax my muscles.

Within the Dream,

as I do in my Nightmares,

I take control of all my thoughts.

I banish all of the supernatural

and subconscious elements completely.

I become wholly aware of reality.

I am able to open my eyes,

which I then do.

I glance at the LED clock at the bedside.

It's 3.15am.

For A Loved One

The sun is bright,
but your eyes are brighter.

The day is light,
but your laugh is lighter.

Kittens play,
but you are more playful.

Music is joy,
but your love is more joyful.

Ice is cold,
your rage is colder.

Fire is hot,
your passion is hotter.

Night is cool,

your smile is cooler.

Dawn is warm,
your embrace is warmer.

Water is clear,
your mind is clearer.

Birds fly high,
our hearts fly higher.

The wind is free.

So are we.

Hub of the Wheel

In this turning world, this spinning top,
we are turning fast, we will never stop;
it turns us off and turns us on,
it's the constant speed we're counting on.
Like a whirling wheel on a phantom car
or a Catherine wheel, or a shooting star,
it turns around in a moment of time
like a carousel in a children's rhyme.

The brightest light in a summer sky,
a piercing gaze from an immortal eye,
it sees us all, can show us why,
it sees us laugh and sees us cry.
A twinkling star, a comet's head,
it guides us where we fear to tread,
a hypnotic arrow with a burning tail,
the wheel spins in the arrow's trail.

We will see our dream at the hub of the wheel

for it has the power to forgive and heal

in a humble trance we will drop and kneel

as our souls all merge at the hub of the wheel

At the hub of the wheel we will all be one

as we melt together in a scorching sun

It's there, it's real

The hub of the wheel

In Death

In Death I am not gone,
just a whisper on the wind.
Singing through the rustling leaves,
at one with Mother as she breathes.

In Death I am still here
on the cooling summer rain,
to wash your tears beside my grave,
together we can both be brave.

In Death I am alive
as I dwell within your soul,
innocent as a new-born lamb,
for you are everything I am.

Lament

A wheelwright toils in the quiet still of dawn,

Crafting proudly as the sparrows call the morning.

Blacksmith pounds iron over anvil,

perfect curves on a simple horseshoe preparing.

A carpenter carefully shapes a candlestick,

waves at passing villagers as he glances from the task.

Farmer works the land as his forefathers did,

Ploughing, harvesting with his Clydesdale companions.

There is nothing but peace

and the country smells on the air.

Sound of machinery

Promise of refinery

Horizon to the future

Advance to prosperity

Banker and architect reshape the skyline in arrogance,

oil and metal gouged from earth with brutal spades.

Steel birds and horses on wasteful merry-go-rounds,
burning in seconds fuels over a million years made.
Scurrying pointlessly, collecting worthless treasures,
artificial focus for those that know no better.
At the end of misdirected lives understanding dawns.
Regrets and sorrow when no more time remains.
There is nothing but rape and damage,
nothing but wasted lives and despair.

Take more than we need,
symbols of violent greed,
abuses of our habitat,
downhill to destruction at alarming speed.

My Girl (A Study in Irony)

There is a girl
I used to laugh and sing with
as the sun shone in the sky.

Our hearts played games
like children smiling.

And then the day
My Girl left me standing,
she never told me why.

And all I know is,
if the Earth turns for a million years
and my spirit is still roaming free,
it will be searching for her.

For I will always love My Girl.

There is a beauty

in the trees and the stars
and the meadows in springtime.
A summer wind, an eagle flying.

But none to touch my angel
and her radiance sublime.

So still I wonder,
as I wander the path of the aimless traveller,
if I shall see that face again
or search in vain forever.

For I will always love My Girl.

Eye of the Storm

Little remains

of iron chains

that manacled my wrists.

Chainsaw

Steel claw

The might of pounding fists.

In the storm's eye

where saints die

and sinners bathe in blood.

No remorse.

Brute force.

To pass through the shadow of history

and chase a secret mystery,

unspeakable banshee in hideous form,

worlds explode in the eye of the storm.

No escape from our destiny,

struck deaf by cacophonous blasphemy,

blinded by the nightmare's form,

retribution in the eye of the storm.

Storm rages

Vague images

on the ceiling of a ruined hall.

A memory dashes

childhood flashes

distant music from behind a wall.

A siren's song

so loud and strong,

choral echoes of a past life.

Narrow ledge

Knife edge

Begin in calamity, end in joy,

wash blood and tears from girl and boy,

have the courage to break the norm;

stare into the eye of the storm.

Utopia, the dream that defies belief;

seek purity of thought in a common thief;

wield the sword,

stay safe and warm,

stab and blind the eye of the storm.

Ephemeral

What separates a flash, a split-second
from a century?
Content, and context.

What separates the life of a woman, or man,
that achieves a million things,
or one monumental thing,
from one that achieves
nothing that anyone remembers?
Content, and context.

What separates those that have lived lives
full of love and happiness
from those that have endured
unfathomable pain and suffering,
and never known a single moment of bliss?
Much, much more than just
content and context.
Everything, the world.

95

Yet in the "scheme of things"

all lives and all experiences

have a beginning,

an end,

and an in-between,

and are gone

as if they never were.

The Psychoabyss

It's a hollowed-out cube of stone.

Somehow there are no cracks or holes,

even at the corners or edges.

I am inside. No light, no air.

My loudest shout, or scream, does not carry.

An unquantifiable, absolute darkness

and silence, is all.

A tangible, palpable, physical

fog of blackness, as if…….

all evil, all pain, all despair

has been fashioned into actual dark matter

that can be felt.

A sludge of material death.

It is real,

yet it transcends

the three dimensions of space
and the single dimension of time.

A perceptible, complete, infinite, eternal void.

It has been formed and created by mind
but it has consumed mind.
Enveloped mind.
Absorbed mind.
Become mind.
And mind has become – it.

Beyond fear, beyond terror,
beyond surrender, and beyond hope.

Magical Eyes

They shine like the distant moon,

they play a song with a haunting tune;

windows to an ocean

into which I gladly fell;

an entrance to Heaven, or was it to Hell?

I was mesmerized.....by those magical eyes.

Black diamonds sparkling brightly,

fiery angel dancing lightly,

we flew briefly together, lighter than air;

your essence lingers everywhere.

I was hypnotised.....y your glistening eyes.

Our souls entwined on a faraway star,

one day again we may reach as far;

Prince and Princess of the universe,

a dream, a wish in which I am immersed.

Purely magnetised.....by those perfect eyes.

Potty Peter Potter & Spotter the Otter

Potty Peter Potter
met an otter in a shop.
The otter bought some butter,
and Peter bought some pop.

"My name is Peter Potter",
said Peter to the otter.
"I see you've bought some butter!"
"Yes I bought it in the shop".

"The weather's getting better",
"Yes it's hotter" said the otter.
"By the way my name is Spotter".
"Pleased to meet you", Peter said.

So Potty Pete and Spotter,
with their pop and pat of butter,
trotted off (as it was hot)
to put the butter in a pot.

Then Peter made a hotpot
out of butter, pop and bread!
"A hotpot out of butter?
That's potty!" Spotter said.

"You're potty, Pete!" said Spotter;
"You're a rotter, Spot!" said Pete.
Then Potty Peter Potter
trotted off home down the street.......!

Mantra

Sagittarius the Fire

Every man's desire

Wizards everywhere

(For those who'd care)

Capricorn the Earth

Stardust from birth

Aquarius the Air

For those who'd care.

My Telepathy

Who shall I fuck with today?
I ask my mind, it just won't say;
smoke a cigarette, heart about to break –
electric tension, too much to take.
But it's all
between me
and my telepathy.

Where will I try to go today?
How am I going to find the way?
Pretty girl jumping through my mind –
I have no map but it's her I must find.
Once again
just the rain
and my telepathy.

Open mind, open window,
open door, open heart.

Ambiguous information,

where do I start?

Which words must I scream today?

Do I run or have the balls to stay?

Broken bones in the alleyway.

Blood on the mirror, come what may.

Come tomorrow, so much sorrow,

all that I can see;

yes it's all

between me

and my telepathy.

The Universal Tree

Three, upon three, upon three.

Beautiful tree, guiding me.

Natural physical trinity.

Tree of infinity.

Triangular chalice of mystery,

atop the tree,

a spirit free.

Clutch the straws of humanity.

Tree of divinity.

Tree of salvation from Eden's soil,

hands of the tree,

lifting me.

Apple's flesh, temptation's spoil.

Tree of all destiny.

Ultimate answer for those with faith,

believe in the tree,

let it be.

Father's arms keeping children safe.

Tree of eternity.

My Epitaph

Here lies Stuart,
as deaf as a post,
as blind as a bat,
as dead as a ghost.

Where lies Stuart
or was he cremated?
Was the moment of death
as he anticipated?

Spiritual Touchdown

The moment we met
I felt a spiritual touchdown.
Bright affinity between our hearts
Magnetic moment

When we first laughed
Spiritual touchdown
Moonbeams lighting up your eyes
Positive and potent

Our first touch
A spiritual touchdown
Waves breaking across my soul
Magical fire

Making love
Beautiful spiritual touchdown
Tremors of love and trust
Real desire

Perfect child

Fruit of spiritual touchdown

Perfect conception in perfect truth

Spiritual child

Spiritual touch

Blood of Gaia

Twisting spire climbs to the skies
as an albatross effortlessly flies.
Earthly creatures crawl and run
as though the world has just begun.

Barracuda darts through water,
seeking minnows for the slaughter.
A python slides from tree to tree
in dreams beyond reality.

Voices sing in harmony,
a choir serenading beauty,
dolphins gliding, singing songs,
revealing where the truth belongs.

A planet, rich in wondrous glory,
telling its own secret story,
its ending could be cloaked in shame,
an incandescent wave of flame.

Or will there be a change of heart?
A phoenix rising, brand new start?
Baptism of a perfect birth,
cleanse the blood of Mother Earth.

………..

Mankind holds the sacred scales
to our own ends of our own tales;
extinction beckons, as we walk
toward the road's ominous fork.

A Hollow Soul

Here, again.

This place, his sanctuary.

This place, his prison.

This place, his tomb.

Dark. Cold, Alone.

Feeling only loss and grief,

surrounded by images of death.

He can only think of death.

His mind unravels like a ball of wool

as he thinks of all the things he loved about her.

Things he will never see or know again.

As he mourns the death of their love,

she is thinking of another.

She is in the arms, the bed, of another.
He is barely a faint, faded memory.

His precious heart and soul
that he willingly gave to her
when their love was fresh, new and beautiful,
scattered to the winds.
His heart an empty, hollow chamber,
nothing but echoes where there once were songs.

A spiritless, blank, emotional vacuum.

Nothing.

House on the Hill

There is a house at the top of the world,

mystical rooms and passages leading to stars.

The door is open to you and me, we could see

the treasures of history, the wonders of near and far

lands and kingdoms. Do you believe it is there?

In the garden, the crisp air is clean and still.

I go there to live through ancient dreams.

A place of beauty, my house on the hill.

The hill rises above life and death,

a blazing beacon lighting the moon and sun.

From the summit, secret places can be seen

where spirits laugh and live as one.

The breeze of dawn blows freely there,

freshest wisdom on sailing winds,

firing the air with magic whispers.

Open your heart, and venture boldly in.

The view is clear from the house on the hill.

Flowers sway, clouds float in the air,
a sight for a humble and questioning eye,
showing that truth is everywhere.
A valley of light summons with flickering flame,
the hill rises high and towers above;
rolling fields of harmony and strength,
glorious waves of everlasting love.

Secret Admirer

I saw her again today.

She smiled at me with her shining eyes.

I'm sure I blushed,
she can't have failed to see it.

She makes me feel like a little boy
playing in the sunshine,
laughing and happy.

My heart beats a little faster
whenever I see her.

Nobody knows about her.

She's my secret.

Key

There's one thing I need
Not a TV or car
Nor a book to read
Just the key to a star.
One key.

A key to the mind
Makes laughter from woe
Gives sight to the blind
Makes a friend from a foe.
One key.

Key to the universe
Everything sweet
Everything worthwhile
A life complete.

Key of positive energy

Unlocks the door for me

The key to love is free

It belongs to humanity.

To you and to me.

One key.

For Sarah

That day,
that May.

That moment
when I first saw your face
and your aura.

That feeling
at that moment
overwhelmed me.

You remember –
I stumbled –
but stayed on my feet
as I ran to you.

My heart didn't burst,
but it felt like it might.

And ever since,

I wanted to –

I needed to –

I had to –

belong to you.

You had lived in my heart,

not only from that day

but all my days before.

It just took a while to find you.

Thank you, Sarah, for completing me.

Love at First Sight?

Do you believe in love at first sight?
If you do not, I think I might.

It may be a crush, it may be true.
I'm not sure what I felt when I first saw you.

For 'You'

I have always been searching

for something unknown.

O'er mountains and valleys

my soul roamed alone.

When my heart burst asunder

I knew it was true;

All of my life

I was searching for you.

In the Dark

I met a girl, and though it was dark,

she was as bright as a button,

as bright as a spark.

Her face was a vision, her beauty divine;

oh how I wish – I wish she were mine!

Forgive Me

Forgive Me
if I think of you all the time,
for I cannot stop
though you'll never be mine;
you're my beautiful dream
on a summer's day,
Forgive Me while I feel this way.

It will certainly pass eventually,
a tragedy, to set it free;
this glowing fire that warms my soul,
Forgive Me while I regain control.

I would surely wait a thousand years
to hold you close and dry your tears.
So if a thousand years it 'be',
Forgive Me if I wait and see.

Kismet

The heat of the sun
gives warmth to the day,
the chill of the night
is like a maiden's call,
if I don't have words
I have nothing to say
and yes, without you
I have nothing at all.

This song is for you
and also for me,
I hope I can find
a place to belong.
I hope that I find
a place to 'be'
and with you in my mind
I can hear this song.

The roll of the river

makes the canyons curl,

the shapes in the stars

say you'll be my girl.

The air that I'm breathing,

it tastes of you,

and the love that I feel,

that love is true.

Ultraviolet

Magical beams from space,
invisible to the human race,
the language of spells and curses,
the trigger when time reverses.

A dog or cat can sense it
and escape its vicious clutch,
a magician will control it
and abuse its tender touch.

Radiation of the soul,
can splinter or make whole,
floating on everyday air,
the rays are everywhere.

Vibrations in each human heart,
one feels them if one tries,
ignorance is bliss, perhaps,
one lives, one loves, one dies.

Seek out those ultraviolet waves
from outer space or from human graves;
spirits or just frequencies?
Maybe psychic dependencies?

Those waves rule the world,
there is no doubt,
believe me or just laugh;
or ask any follower of the Left Hand Path.

Elephant

The trunk of the elephant
is long and thin and grey;
it really is so very big
it must get in the way?

He has the very longest nose
you ever could believe.
But isn't it a wonderful nose
with which to breathe?

He also has four thick, round feet
to help him stand up straight;
he's so damn big and heavy
that you'd think he would need eight.

Elephants have big ears too,
and tusks as long as tails.
And they remember everything,
their memory never fails.

129

So if you see an elephant

be sure to say hello.......

He'll remember you for ever,

THAT you'll always know!

Animal Magic

It's raining today.
Raining cats and dogs?
My mistake,
it's lions and wolves.

I stood in front of a running rhino.
I thought he'd flatten me
but he just ran past.
Anyway, he can't run fast.

I spoke to a dolphin, with my mind.
He spoke back, he was very kind.

An elephant trod on a snake.
Oops, it's dead.
Due to its flattened head.

A man trod on a scorpion.

Oops, he got stung.

Silly thing to have done.

The magic of animals.

Take heed.

They are watching our greed.

They can make us bleed.

Let's not start a stampede.

Mathematical Mountain

I was always a clever little shit.

An unhealthily and annoyingly bright boy.

Reading broadsheets on demand at age three,

show-off party pieces,

and slowly, but surely,

the natural appendage of arrogance

grafted itself onto my ugly psyche.

Hand always first into the air,

and also very well aware

why the teachers made a point of ignoring mine,

and allowing the limelight to generally shine

upon as many other kids as was possible.

Even when I understood

the rules of the neighbourhood,

it was impossible to resist

the urges of the narcissist.

It's all very well being clever and smart,
but getting it down to a science, or an art,
that's something very much more profound
to try and grasp.

Arrogance precipitates complacency,
so misconceptions at that end of the scale
lay one at risk of multiple, embarrassing screw-ups.
Even if they are relatively rare,
they're uncomfortable.
Egos are all the more precious to the egotistical.

But at the other end of the spectrum,
the manifestation of the (less frequent) humility.

Humility precipitates doubt, and fear,
and an even more battered pride.
Perhaps the more dangerous of the two extremes.
Or so it often seems.
After some years of having my intellect praised,
and my profile undeservingly raised,

134

after victory and prestige,

silly, overstated recognition based on

the narrowest of measurements,

came a time when I met my match

in no uncertain way.

Having rarely had to break a sweat

in an academic arena,

I decided I was worthy of being one of the

"top 1% of the top 1%",

or at least that's how they like to sell it.

My humble grammar school, up against

the might of the posh contingent.

Those that come from the right families,

that have the right historical bloodlines

and the right access to the right establishments.

How dare we,

the state school pretenders,

try to compete on that ridiculously, steeply sloped

playing field?

Anyway, I and my unearned genius label
had committed ourselves.

An application to the University of Oxford
to study Chemistry.
I had been declared,
by way of the school prize, no less,
the best in our illustrious school
at that specified discipline.
I had my 'A' Grade at 'A' Level
and my 'Special Paper' Distinction
under my belt already at that stage.
I had my 'A' Grade in Physics too.

But my Achilles' Heel had made itself
glaringly apparent,
the shock of the 'C' in my 'A' Level Mathematics.
My complacent arrogance that I spoke of before
had bitten me, hard, on my fat arse.

At Oxford, as you would expect,
they had noticed it.

And so, as well as my shiny 'A' grades,
and my Distinction,
it was, as it were, "so what?"

That's all very well, Stuart, you're a clever chap,
but what you have displayed
is by no means conclusive enough.

We would like you to sit the 'General Paper'
which will require you to demonstrate – in
addition to your scientific mastery –
the ability to write, comprehensively,
on matters of ethics, philosophy, politics,
and analysis of related topics.

And then, of course, you will need to sit a
Mathematics paper,
because you have not convinced us

of your suitability level in that area.

I sat my General Paper.

Without really any certainty
of whether I had shown anything
that was required.

My Chemistry papers, of which there were two,
both at a higher level of difficulty
than 'A' Level questions,
were comfortable to endure.

I had worked through some past years' papers
in Chemistry, Maths and the General Paper,
but for maybe the first time in my entire life
I doubted whether I had delivered
what I had needed to.
And then,
I found myself in the room for the
Mathematics exam.

The subject that I was supposed to be
very good at, but had recently been
demonstrating that I wasn't.

It didn't actually matter how
'Supercalifragilisticexpialidocious'
I was at everything else,
if I screwed up the Maths exam.
For perhaps the first time in my
silly, young, inexperienced, big-headed life,

I was under real pressure;
and I was looking abject defeat and failure
right in the eye.

If I had ever felt true fear, it was then.

The exam's duration was three hours.
I had achieved a 'C' in my 'A' Level
which was of a far less difficult standard.

I looked through the questions.

I cannot remember exactly,

but there were, say,

ten or twelve questions,

each from a different branch of mathematics –

none of which I was particularly adept at.

I had to choose and answer, say, six or seven of them.

So, I read through them,

in theory, to decide which I could best attempt.

Exam technique in such a situation

being to get the brain engaged

by answering the one that I felt

most confident about.

I read them through, carefully, once.

Then again, this time concentrating hard,

thinking which methods were needed to

solve each of them.

More than a whole hour passed,

of only three that I had,

and my pen had not touched the paper.

Everyone else in the room,

(there were about seven of us)

had been writing since about the ten-minute point.

I was, internally, frantic.

Pure panic,

my entire life seemed to be

focused on these very moments,

and it seemed to be dragging me

into the bowels of Hell.

Fortunately, I do not believe in Hell.

Somehow or other, shortly into the second hour,

I realised the method to attack one of the questions.

So I answered it.

Like a stiff muscle into a training session,

my brain seemed to open up and work.

Mathematics is about method, memory, logic.
The more I did, the faster my mind worked,
and I was in a hurry.
Two hours in which to try and do three hours' work.
I scribbled and looked constantly at the time.

By the end, as I recall,
I did produce the number of solutions
I'd been asked for.
I was by no means happy that I had passed the exam,
but I was happy that I had given it a fair shot.

Like many, I genuinely felt that I might be either
accepted or rejected, despite a lifetime of
successes at all my academic endeavours.

And so the December Saturday morning,
when my acceptance letter hit the doormat,
galvanised one of the most serious lessons
that I have ever learned, to this day,
thirty-seven years on.

142

Tower of Stone

Heroes have tried to enter,
but the walls are of stone.

The tower was made when time began
from the mightiest stone.

Heathen warriors hammer and batter,
but their weapons are powerless.

The treasures within are not for a barbarian's eyes.
Entrance forever denied,
an impregnable fortress to mortal beings.

The way in.......

dissolve into particles,
very molecules of thought,
spread into mistcloud,
move through the stone,

through the stone.

It is welcoming,

drawing in,

magnetic, pulling upward,

a staircase,

a skyward spiralling coil,

drift in,

drift up,

drift in,

drift up.

Climb above the sky,

above the stars,

float.......rise.......

a chamber,

a cavernous hall,

songs.......

Musical Truths,

Mathematical Truths,

Philosophical Truths,

Spiritual Truths.

My being.......

All beings.......

My form,

my face,

changing, moving,

melting, merging.

Woman, man,

child, spirit,

fish, bird, tree,

lion, tiger, wolf, bear,

wind, rain, river, mountain, forest,

thunder, lightning,

hurricane's eye,

natural power,

unnatural power,

all power,

smiling, crying,

showing, teaching,

shining, sharing, caring,

loving,

wisdom, faith, hope,

TRUTH.

Pure love,

sun, moon, ocean, sky, star,

time, space,

all merging,

becoming one,

pure consciousness,

all consciousness,

one essence,

bathe in the essence,

join with the essence,

I am the essence,

we are the essence,

everything is the essence,

bathe in the essence,

become the essence,

be the essence,

bathe in the essence,

the universal essence,

bathe,

bathe,

bathe.

Printed in Great Britain
by Amazon